Your Amazing Body

Hands

by Imogen Kingsley

Bullfrog Books

Ideas for Parents and Teachers

Bullfrog Books let children practice reading informational text at the earliest reading levels. Repetition, familiar words, and photo labels support early readers.

Before Reading

- Discuss the cover photo. What does it tell them?
- Look at the picture glossary together. Read and discuss the words.

Read the Book

- "Walk" through the book and look at the photos. Let the child ask questions. Point out the photo labels.
- Read the book to the child, or have him or her read independently.

After Reading

- Prompt the child to think more. Ask: Think of all the ways you use your hands. What would be the hardest thing to do without hands?

Bullfrog Books are published by Jump!
5357 Penn Avenue South
Minneapolis, MN 55419
www.jumplibrary.com

Library of Congress Cataloging-in-Publication Data

Names: Kingsley, Imogen, author.
Title: Hands / by Imogen Kingsley.
Description: Minneapolis, MN: Jump! [2017]
Series: Your amazing body | Audience: Ages 5–8.
Includes bibliographical references and index.
Identifiers: LCCN 2016048925 (print)
LCCN 2016049095 (ebook)
ISBN 9781620316863 (hardcover: alk. paper)
ISBN 9781620317396 (pbk.)
ISBN 9781624965630 (ebook)
Subjects: LCSH: Hand—Juvenile literature.
Anatomy—Juvenile literature.
Classification: LCC QM548 .K5254 2017 (print)
LCC QM548 (ebook) | DDC 612.9/7—dc23
LC record available at https://lccn.loc.gov/201604892

Editor: Jenny Fretland VanVoorst
Book Designer: Molly Ballanger
Photo Researcher: Molly Ballanger

Photo Credits: age fotostock: Heiner Heine, 5. Getty: Blue Images, 9; Mike Kemp, 10–11; OPIFICIO 42, 18. Shutterstock: karelnoppe, cover; bernashafo, 1; OnlyZoia, 3; Elena Stepanova, 4; Ilike, 6–7; Cherednychenko Ihor, 8; wittaya changkaew, 12–13; Linda Bucklin, 16–17; Matthias G. Ziegler, 16–17; PhotoSerg, 16–17; Rock and Wasp, 20–21; AGNDAM _ Ai, 22; alexandre zveiger, 22; cristi180884, 22; Sebastian Kaulitzki, 23tl, 23tr, 23br; Alexander Mazurevich, 23. SuperStock: Blend Images, 14–15, 19.

Printed in the United States of America at Corporate Graphics in North Mankato, Minnesota.

Table of Contents

Hands are handy.

What can they do?

hammer

Hands grab.

Kai holds a fork.

Joe uses a hammer.

Hands touch.
JD pets his cat.

Ava tickles her brother.

Hands work.

Max writes a letter.

Kim makes a hat.

11

Hands play.

Jed throws a ball.

Ann plays the piano.

Hands are amazing!

How do they work?

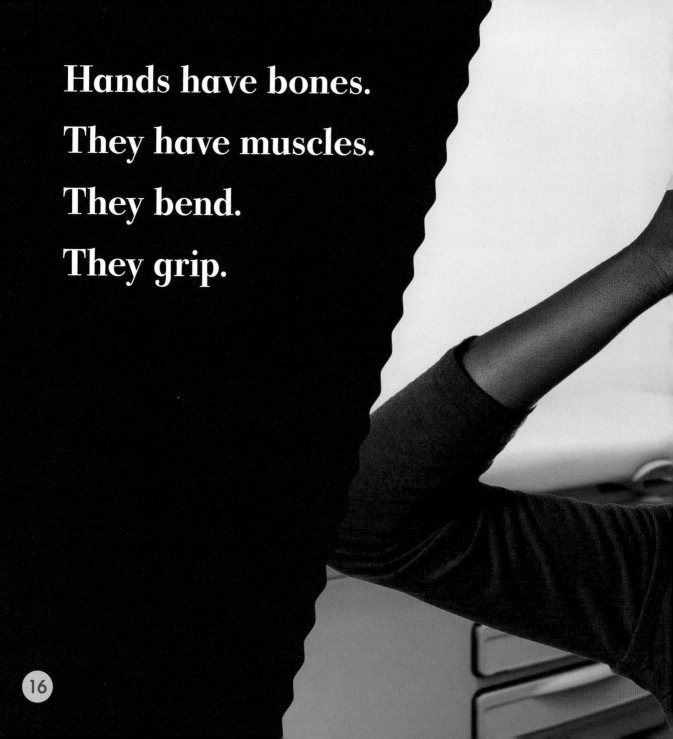

Hands have bones.

They have muscles.

They bend.

They grip.

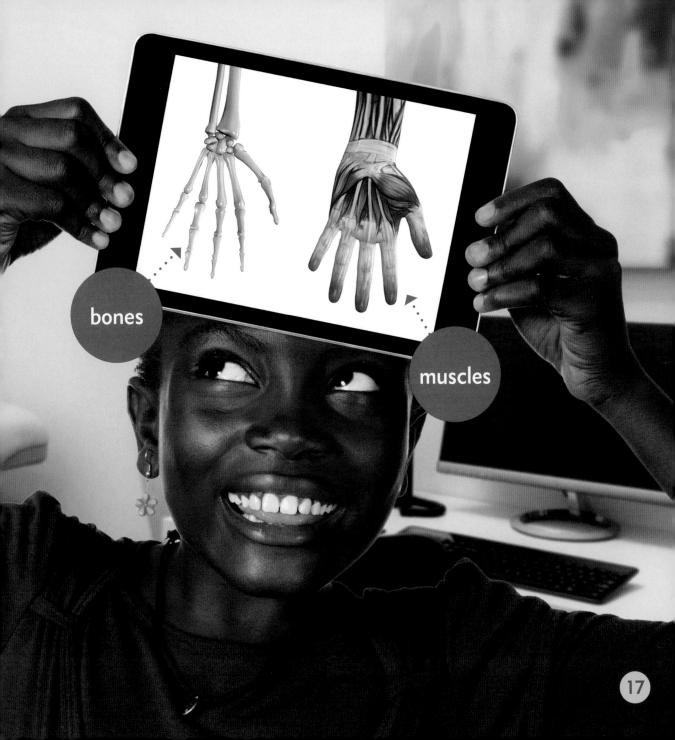

bones

muscles

Hands have nerves.

They feel.

Is it wet? Is it dry?

It is soft? Is it hard?

Hands are handy!

What can your hands do?

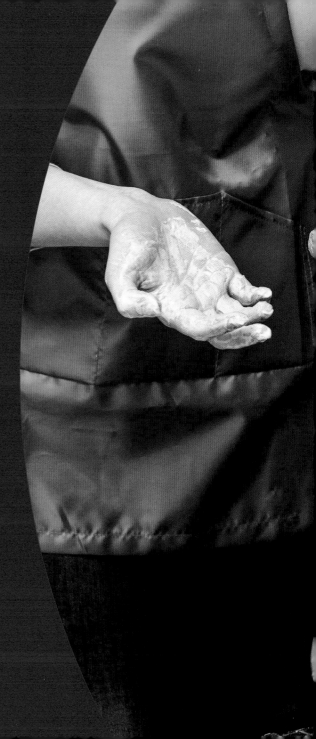

Parts of the Hand

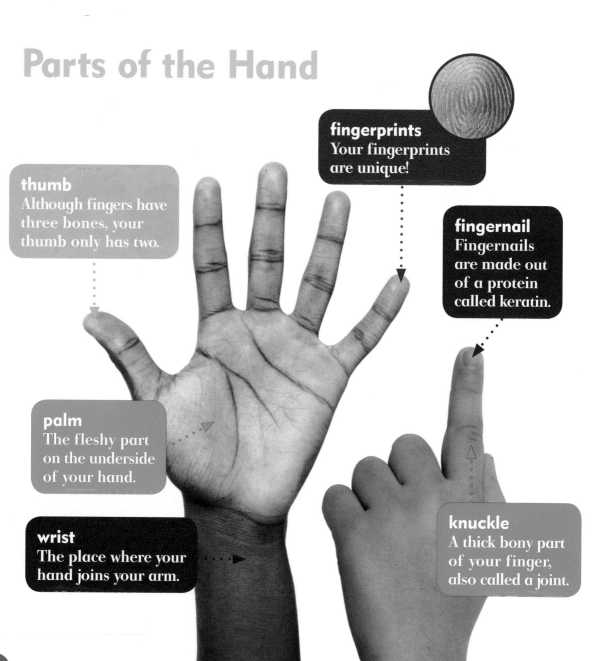

fingerprints
Your fingerprints are unique!

thumb
Although fingers have three bones, your thumb only has two.

fingernail
Fingernails are made out of a protein called keratin.

palm
The fleshy part on the underside of your hand.

wrist
The place where your hand joins your arm.

knuckle
A thick bony part of your finger, also called a joint.

Picture Glossary

bones
The hard pieces in your body that make up your frame; your hand has 27 bones.

muscles
The parts of your body that make movement.

handy
Useful.

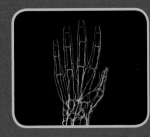

nerves
Small parts in your body that carry messages to the brain and other parts of your body.

Index

To Learn More

Learning more is as easy as 1, 2, 3.

1) Go to www.factsurfer.com

2) Enter "hands" into the search box.

3) Click the "Surf" button to see a list of websites.

With factsurfer.com, finding more information is just a click away.

24